D0573734

# OPERATION SIBERIAN CRANE

## The Story Behind the
## International Effort to Save an Amazing Bird

# OPERATION SIBERIAN CRANE

### The Story Behind the
### International Effort to Save an Amazing Bird

by
## Judi Friedman

**DILLON PRESS**
New York

Maxwell Macmillan Canada
Toronto
Maxwell Macmillan International
New York   Oxford   Singapore   Sydney

This book is dedicated to Ron Sauey, whose warmth, humor, hard work, and caring helped to create the world-famous International Crane Foundation.

## Acknowledgments

Special thanks to George Archibald, the International Crane Foundation, and Vladimir Flint, whose trust, time, energy, and resources helped to create this book. Final words of gratitude go to Viatcheslav Slouzhivov, formerly of the Soviet Peace Committee in Moscow, and to Howard and Alice Frazier of Promoting Enduring Peace, Woodmont, Connecticut, whose generosity made this work possible.

## Photo Credits

All photos courtesy of ICF except: David Thompson, 8; Judi Friedman, 54; Steven Landfried, 61

### Library of Congress Cataloging-in Publication Data

Friedman, Judi, 1935-
    Operation Siberian crane : the story behind the international effort to save an amazing bird / by Judi Friedman. — 1st ed.
        p.   cm.
    Includes bibliographical references and index.
    Summary: Describes the cooperative effort by scientists in the Soviet Union and the United States to save the Siberian crane, with the support and aid of conservationists from other nations.
    ISBN 0-87518-515-0
    1. Siberian crane—Juvenile literature. 2. Birds, Protection of—International cooperation—Juvenile literature. 3. Rare birds—Juvenile literature. 4. International Crane Foundation—Juvenile literature. [1. Siberian crane. 2. Cranes. 3. Birds—Protection. 4. Rare birds. 5. International Crane Foundation. 6. Wildlife conservation.] I. Title.
QL696.G84F75    1992
639.9'7831—dc20                                                      92-13775

Dillon Press                                  Maxwell Macmillan Canada, Inc.
Macmillan Publishing Company                  1200 Eglinton Avenue East
866 Third Avenue                              Suite 200
New York, NY  10022                           Don Mills, Ontario M3C 3N1

Macmillan Publishing Company is part of the Maxwell Communication Group of Companies.

First edition

Printed in the United States of America

10  9  8  7  6  5  4  3  2  1

# Contents

Foreword..................................................................6

Range of the Siberian Crane..............................7

1. A Rare and Beautiful Bird..........................9

2. Two Americans.........................................15

3. A Home for Cranes...................................22

4. Operation Siberian Crane........................28

5. Russian Eggs in America..........................35

6. Aeroflot and Friends................................45

7. A New Home in Russia.............................50

8. Migrating through Afghanistan and Pakistan..........57

9. Wintering in India and Iran......................62

10. Wonderful News in China........................67

11. American and Soviet Offspring................73

12. Symbols of Hope....................................77

Glossary..................................................................86

Chronology...........................................................88

Bibliography..........................................................91

Index.......................................................................94

# Foreword

This book is about trying to save a beautiful bird, one that, tragically, has become endangered. It is also about people overcoming tremendous obstacles of geographic separation, difficult communications, prejudice, ignorance, and the haunting effects of poverty and war.

It is the story of friendships forged during the cold war and of tireless men and women working to create an environment that can sustain all the creatures that inhabit our fragile planet.

*Operation Siberian Crane* stands as a reminder that mutual trust and common goals can unite caring people from all parts of the globe. . .our only hope for solving the environmental crisis that confronts us all.

**—John A. Hoyt**
Chief Executive, The Humane Society of the United States
President, EarthKind International

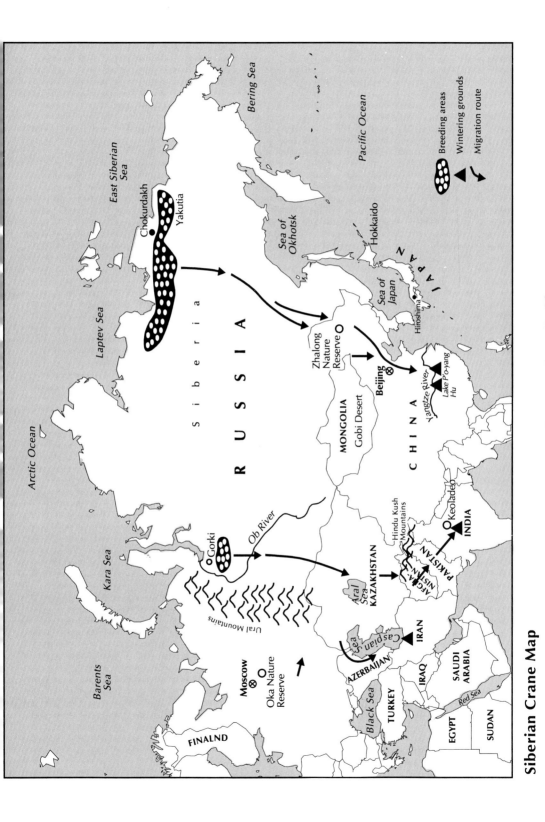

**Siberian Crane Map**

# CHAPTER 1

# A RARE AND
# BEAUTIFUL BIRD

Imagine a thin white bird, almost as tall as you are, with great black-tipped wings that can span eight feet and carry it over high mountains at top speed. This is the majestic Siberian crane, a bird that people have called "poetry in motion" because its movements are so slow, deliberate, and graceful. It is an intense bird, with startling yellow eyes gazing out of a reddish pink unfeathered face.

Cranes dance. They create breathtaking spectacles that begin as the birds throw sticks, catch them, drop them, pick them up, and then leap into the air to a height of eight to ten feet. They move backward with jumps and side whirls, throwing their heads high, legs slightly bent. Their immense wings wave or hang motionless. Cranes dance at any age and in any season, although they seem to dance most often before breeding. The dancing is so inspiring that since ancient times peoples of many cultures have copied the birds' movements in their own dances.

Equal to the elegant grace of the Siberian crane is its special voice, which can be heard from almost a mile away on a still day. Its soft, flutelike tones float down like music from the sky long before the bird can be seen. Siberian

*The elegant Siberian crane—often called "the snow-wreath" because of its pure white coat.*

cranes call continuously when they fly during migration, heralds of the change of seasons.

Another very unusual kind of song can be heard when the male and female birds call together. The male begins his song; then the female crane blends in so perfectly that the two calls sound like the voice of a single bird. Every year, pairs of birds across the vast Siberian tundra dance and call together.

Long ago the ancestors of the Siberian crane covered the earth in great flocks. For 54 million years, they stalked many of the marshes of the world. Today there are 15 species of crane. They are found in all parts of the world except South America, the Malayan Islands, Polynesia, New Zealand, and Antarctica.

Cranes have fascinated people for centuries. Deep inside a cave in southern Spain there is a drawing of a single crane staring at its nest. It was painted by a Stone Age man 6,000 years ago. The ancient tomb of Ti in Egypt shows an accurate picture of two different kinds of cranes.

Russian tradition celebrates the crane's loyalty. Siberian cranes display this quality by staying with the same mate year after year, by taking very good care of their chicks, and by returning to the same places each year during and after long migrations. Old Russian songs refer to cranes as the souls of soldiers returning steadfastly to their homeland.

The crane is also admired for its long life. One Siberian

*Male and female Eurasian cranes "unison call." Their two voices blend so perfectly together that they sound like the call of a single bird.*

crane at the National Zoo in Washington, D.C., for instance, lived for 61 years. Wolf, a crane whose age was estimated at 82, died at the International Crane Foundation in Wisconsin in 1987. He is listed in the *Guinness Book of World Records* as the world's oldest living bird. Because of the cranes' longevity, the Japanese display pictures and statues of cranes at their marriage and birth ceremonies.

They are symbols of a healthy, prosperous, and happy life . . . a life without war. Therefore, cranes have also become symbols of peace.

The Siberian crane, scientific name *Grus leucogeranus*, is one of the most magnificent members of the crane family. Its pure white body and black-tipped wings have earned it the nicknames "the snow-wreath," "the lily of birds," and "the crane with long black sleeves." A Sibe, as it is affectionately called, can weigh up to 18 pounds when fully grown and have a wingspan of eight feet.

As its name suggests, the Siberian crane is born in isolated regions of Siberia in northern Russia. It makes its home on a marshy, treeless plain called the tundra. This is where, during the spring and summer, it breeds and raises its chicks. Its nests can be found in two small, widely separate areas in eastern and western Siberia (see map on page 7). During the freezing winter, the birds in western Siberia migrate to warmer Iran and India, traveling through Azerbaijan, Kazakhstan, Afghanistan, and Pakistan, and the cranes in eastern Siberia migrate to southern China. Both breeding and wintering ranges used to be much larger in the 18th and 19th centuries, but have shrunk drastically, along with the crane population, in the last hundred years.

Today cranes are one of the most threatened groups of animals in the world. Seven of the fifteen different species of cranes are endangered. The Siberian crane is one of the most endangered of these seven species. Its name is listed in Russia's Red Book—a special book that lists endangered species and urges protection of them. The color red signals the danger of extinction for these rare creatures.

The disappearance of even one living thing is cause for alarm. Its loss may mean that something in nature is out of order, out of balance. Its loss may also affect the animals or plants that it eats, the animals that eat it, or the place in which it grows . . . for everything is connected. The disappearance of even a tiny kind of insect or fish should make people ask "Why?"

The Siberian crane has become an endangered species for a number of reasons. Both its breeding and wintering grounds have shrunk and are in constant danger of being further destroyed by human expansion. To live, Siberian cranes depend on very special feeding areas—expanses of safe and unpolluted wetlands where they can find the roots of submerged plants. For centuries wetlands remained undisturbed because people did not have the equipment to drain them; now they do. These shallow-water habitats are being turned into fields for planting and grazing, thereby crowding the Sibes into what few wetlands remain. There they must compete with other birds for food and are easier prey for all kinds of enemies—especially hunters.

Siberian cranes are especially ready targets because of

their immense size and snow-white color. Their constant communication also makes their presence obvious. Loyalty between the pairs and among the families is another problem. If one bird is shot, its mate will remain near the dead or injured crane and often be shot itself. Even today hunters stalk the birds as they migrate through mountain passes and rest in wetlands.

Because the Siberian crane travels through so many different countries and regions during its 3,000 to 5,000 mile migration, it is very difficult to enforce laws to protect it. No one country can save this magnificent white bird. It was not until the 1970s, after years of hostility and suspicion, that scientists from the United States and the Soviet Union launched the international effort to save the endangered Siberian crane.

# CHAPTER 2

# TWO AMERICANS

Fortunately for cranes, there are people who love them. One of these people was a dark-haired, gentle young man with a wonderful sense of humor named Ron Sauey. As a child he had collected butterflies; then his parents helped him build an aviary so he could raise pheasants. In 1971 Ron met George Archibald at Cornell University, where they were both studying. Their common love of cranes brought them together in a special way. The two men decided that they would work to try to save cranes all over the world. The International Crane Foundation was born.

Ron's parents, Claire and Norman Sauey, provided the place—their then-vacant 65-acre horse farm in central Wisconsin. Because cranes can endure cold weather, the location was excellent. The price was right, too. Ron's parents leased the farm to Ron and George for $1.00! The new International Crane Foundation (ICF) had a real home. It began with a few simple cages in 1972.

The foundation's purpose was to become a world center for the study and preservation of cranes. The center would help to coordinate crane research and breed captive birds in hopes of returning some of them to the wild. The foundation also took on the job of educating the public, helping to pass new national and international laws, and helping to enforce existing laws. Most importantly, it located and then helped to preserve safe, appropriate areas for each crane species.

Crane eggs and adult birds of every species had to be brought to ICF. Once there, the birds could be bred. Their offspring would become a "genetic bank." Then the particular characteristics of a particular species from a certain area would not be lost if that species died in the wild. Eggs and young adult birds could be taken to new, potentially safe areas or to places where the cranes had once thrived. However, to be successful in these final stages, every aspect of captive breeding had to be understood and satisfactorily completed.

George Archibald and Ron Sauey did everything they could to educate themselves in the behavior of cranes. While George was at Cornell University, he examined the comparative behavior of various species of cranes. By collecting these birds from zoos and by traveling to habitats all over the world, he was able to study all but two species—one of which was the Siberian crane. In the late 1960s and early 1970s, few Sibes were held in captivity. Strained relations between the United States and the Soviet Union made it difficult to study them in Russia, and China was still closed to foreigners. The birds seemed to have disappeared from Iran, a traditional wintering place.

With the establishment of ICF, George's traveling increased. He worked diligently in Australia, Korea, and Japan. For many months of the year, his home was almost the entire globe. His work provided him with unusual experiences. While searching for the Eastern sarus crane, he tramped through the swamps of Australia during the heavy rainy season in 100°F heat. To find the nests of the cranes that lived there, he hiked through 10 to 15 miles of swamps full of poisonous snakes and huge leeches. When George saw a bird suddenly stand up, then he would know a nest was nearby. George would take only one egg from the nest for his new captive breeding center.

In Korea, George went looking for red-crowned cranes. He found them. The cranes were resting in the two-and-a-half-mile demilitarized zone between North and South Korea, a dangerous, no-man's-land. To reach these birds, George had to walk along paths through mine fields. Because of George's deep caring and hard work, he finally convinced the government of South Korea to create a nature reserve on 30 square miles of marshland in this very unusual place.

George also went to Japan and found that Japanese cranes did not migrate, as everyone had thought. Instead, he discovered, all the cranes that wintered near a remote marsh area in southeastern Hokkaido also bred there. His discovery helped lead to the preservation of the marsh, thereby ensuring the safety of these birds.

While George Archibald spent his time studying many different species of cranes, his codirector, Ron Sauey, concentrated on just one—the Siberian crane. He began his pioneering work during his doctoral study of this little-known crane species. His new classroom was the only known winter home of the Siberian crane—a large wetland in north-central India. Named Keoladeo Ghana Bird Sanctuary, it is located in Bharatpur, Rajasthan. Here 11½ square miles of marsh and woodland provide food and shelter for 374 species of birds.

Although hunting was not allowed in the sanctuary, Ron knew that the small population of Siberian cranes that wintered there was decreasing. Perhaps by constantly observing the cranes, Ron could learn facts that might save these beautiful birds from disappearing forever.

Habib, the cook at the sanctuary rest house where Ron stayed, thought Ron was rather strange. Here was a man who spent all day sitting in the middle of the marshes. At 5:00 in the dark, cold winter mornings, Ron would pack his tape recorder, telescope, binoculars, and tripod and stumble out into the darkness to bicycle to his "little home" in the marshes, a small island platform covered by

*Sunrise at Keoladeo Ghana Bird Sanctuary, a large wetland in north-central India*

a bamboo frame and mounds of dried plants. Since the platform was 100 yards from the nearest dry land, Ron had to change into shorts and walk through murky water to reach it. Then he would sit, observing the great drama around him.

As the dull red glow of sunrise deepened, owls hooted. The calls of nesting stork chicks, herons, ibis, spoonbills, and other birds increased. An air of expectancy hung over the shallow lake. Then the flutelike calls of the approaching Sibes drifted down from the sky. The different pitches of the male and female birds made a strange and wondrous harmony. Sometimes white parent birds with their white-and-brown chick settled close to Ron. "Then I stopped breathing for a while," he said.

*Keoladeo is home to 374 species of birds. Ron Sauey concentrated on just one—the Siberian crane, and his research brought to light many new and important facts necessary to the bird's survival.*

Ron would sit for hours at a time each day, watching the cranes eat, sleep, relax, and clean and protect themselves. By March the cranes would begin to move around more and more, making short flights as they readied for their perilous journey back to the ice-covered breeding grounds of Siberia in western Russia. For Ron their departure meant his return to Baraboo, Wisconsin.

Ron revisited Keoladeo for six winters over a ten-year period. His research proved for the first time that in the winter months the Siberian crane exists primarily on a specialized diet of water plants. Its massive beak extracts the roots and tubers of sedges, plants that grow in muddy marshlands. Unlike other crane species, Siberian cranes cannot find food on dry land or even dig in semidry mud. The mud must be covered by at least a little water—a very specialized condition that is one more factor in threatening the crane's survival.

CHAPTER 3

# A HOME FOR CRANES

**W**hen Ron and George were not traveling, they were expanding the International Crane Foundation headquarters in Baraboo. ICF is a beautiful place. Low, earth-colored buildings and bird enclosures rest amid the rolling hills of central Wisconsin. Although the pens were planned to house a variety of crane species, both George and Ron became especially concerned about the fate of the Siberian cranes. They knew the Soviets believed that the eastern Siberian flock was declining. No one even knew where this flock wintered, although they suspected the locale was in China. Mao Zedong, China's leader, did not believe that nature conservation was important. In fact, in 1959 the nation had tried to kill all its sparrows. In India, Ron had observed that fewer Sibes were coming to the wintering grounds there; and no one knew where in western Siberia this flock bred. In addition, cranes were hunted in Afghanistan and Pakistan as they migrated through the mountains.

ICF contacted all the zoos that housed Siberian cranes. Only seven adult Sibes were held in captivity. Four were sent to Baraboo over a two-year period for breeding. ICF was a good home to the first two Siberian cranes who came in 1976 on loan—an older female named Philis, from the Philadelphia Zoo, and a 71-year-old male named Wolf, from a bird park called Vogelpark Walsrode in northern West Germany. These two Sibes shared a pen.

Ron and George believed that they knew why Siberian cranes had never bred in captivity. The periods of light in the mid-latitudes were shorter than the continuous light of May and June in the Arctic tundra. Floodlights controlled by a time clock were put near the pen of Philis and Wolf. Starting in mid-March, about the dates that the cranes would usually leave their warm winter feeding grounds, the birds were exposed to longer and longer periods of artificial light—just as if they were flying to the northern wilds. Eventually 22 hours of light brightened the noisy pen.

In her first season with Wolf, Philis laid 12 eggs! She had never laid an egg before in her 30 years of captivity. However, old Wolf did not seem to be fertile; the eggs never hatched.

Soon the two ICF Sibes were joined by another. Some years earlier, in 1969, a young Siberian crane had been found in a ditch in Japan by a high-school student. Exhausted and unable to run away, the young brown-and-white bird was starving. It had probably been separated from its parents as it flew from the Siberian

tundra to some unknown wintering grounds in China. The crane had been named Hirakawa because it had been given to the Hirakawa Zoo. This precious bird was lent to the International Crane Foundation because the Japanese knew and trusted George. They deeply respected the work that he had done to help save the Japanese red-crowned crane in the Hokkaido marshes.

Breeding cranes is a difficult business. Wild cranes separate into pairs during the breeding season. These pairs are aggressive and protective, sometimes even driving away large animals like reindeer from their nests on the Siberian tundra. Believing Hirakawa to be a male—perhaps a fertile one—the workers at ICF put the young crane in a pen near Wolf.

One of the major problems in breeding Sibes is the difficulty in telling a female from a male; the two sexes look almost exactly alike. However, when the cranes make their unison call, the male bird usually raises his wings more than the female. Females also give higher and more rapid calls. The voice of Hirakawa immediately showed the ICF workers what sex she was! Wolf became excited and extremely aggressive; he attacked and killed the only crane who couldn't escape him, Philis, who was in his cage. Ron, George, and other ornithologists (bird scientists) learned a hard lesson. No longer could all pairs be placed in the same pen. Even though the scientists

*Wolf and Philis, the first Siberian cranes brought to ICF*

now knew that Hirakawa was a female, they didn't dare put her in the same cage with Wolf. The cranes were put in adjoining cages. Of course, birds in separate pens cannot get together to mate, so workers at ICF had to assist with the mating process.

They used artificial insemination, a scientific way of breeding. They began early in the morning, when the birds seemed ready. A worker familiar to the male held him, firmly but gently stroking his thighs until he relaxed. As the crane raised his tail, he released semen into a glass held by another helper. Meanwhile, the back of the female was stroked. When she relaxed and raised her tail, and began to make a purring sound, a worker gently injected her with the semen. Artificial insemination was done about every three days. Some semen was also frozen, to be used at a later date or to be sent to other zoos around the world.

By using artificial insemination, semen can be obtained from cranes who may have been injured or who are missing a wing, preventing them from mating normally. Sending semen to zoos or other breeding centers ensures that each new baby crane will have a variety of genes. A diverse genetic biology produces hardier birds that can adapt to more environmental changes. They also may be able to resist disease more successfully, thus helping the species to survive.

Besides providing long hours of daylight, ICF workers improved breeding conditions by making changes in the birds' diet. Although in winter cranes are mostly vegetarian, breeding cranes eat a lot of meat. Wild birds arriving on the tundra catch small animals like frogs, fish, and lemmings. So in captivity more protein was added to the breeding crane's diet, signaling to its body that something was happening.

Nesting materials of sticks and grasses were also provided. The Siberian cranes danced, tossing these materials into the air. Old Wolf built nest after nest along the wires separating him from Hirakawa, thus encouraging his fertility and accelerating her egg laying. It was hoped that as Hirakawa became older and more used to Wolf, the two cranes would stimulate each other and the process of artificial insemination would prove successful.

CHAPTER 4

# OPERATION SIBERIAN CRANE

In order to have a truly successful breeding program, the scientists at ICF knew that they would need the cooperation of the Soviet government. Only in the Soviet Union did wild Siberian cranes lay the eggs that George and Ron needed to raise Siberian cranes in captivity. But since the end of World War II, the United States and the Soviet Union had been engaged in a cold war: a war of words and threats, but not actual fighting. The two countries piled up bombs to use in case of real war, until eventually they had 50,000 nuclear weapons aimed at each other.

In this frightening political climate, there was little cultural or scientific exchange between the two countries during the 1950s and 1960s. But in 1972 the United States and the Soviet Union agreed to cooperate on environmental projects. This agreement made it possible in 1975 for George and Ron to send a letter to Dr. Vladimir Flint, a Russian ornithologist, who had been working to save the crane in the Soviet Union.

A large man with a wonderful smile and graying blond hair, Vladimir had liked "all living creatures ... frogs, insects, everything" even when he was a very small child. As he grew older, he began to study animal diseases and, because he loved birds, he began to collect bird eggs.

"Birds' eggs are like shells, one of the most beautiful things on the planet," said Vladimir. "A person doesn't really know a bird until he can find its nest. Birds hide their nests so well that if you find an egg, it proves you know the bird and its habits."

Years earlier Vladimir had gone to the remote region of Yakutia in eastern Siberia. Traveling by foot, horseback, and cross-country vehicle and always wearing a cap, he studied animal diseases and collected birds' eggs in his spare time. "At that time collecting eggs seemed okay," he said. "No one knew about endangered species." Dr. Flint found a rare Siberian crane nest holding two big, warm, greenish eggs with red-brown spots. Later he said, "I was the luckiest man alive. I did not yet know that fate would link me with those birds for years to come."

Year after year he returned to the tundra and observed Siberian cranes. He became fascinated by the amazing birds. Not only were they enormous and beautiful, but they also seemed to care for one another and for their chicks. He found their cries hauntingly beautiful.

In March 1976, at the invitation of Vladimir Flint, George Archibald went to Moscow, where he was met by Libby Anderson, a Cornell student who was ICF's

volunteer Russian expert. The two Americans talked for hours with Vladimir and many Soviet officials about an extraordinary project: transporting Siberian crane eggs from the Soviet Union to the United States. They also discussed putting Siberian crane eggs into the nests of another kind of crane—the more plentiful Eurasian crane that wintered in Iran.

A daring new agreement was signed by the two countries. It said that six eggs from wild Siberian cranes could be flown from the tundra of eastern Siberia to central Wisconsin in the United States—traveling three-quarters of the way around the world. Siberian cranes usually lay two eggs but raise only one chick. Thus, the scientists reasoned, it would be all right to take one egg from each nest.

If the Siberian crane eggs survived this long journey, then the hatched baby cranes might live and grow and breed. And later, if the grown-up females laid fertile eggs, these eggs could travel back to Moscow. From there they could be placed in Eurasian crane nests to hatch. These Siberian chicks would go with their Eurasian crane foster parents to their wintering grounds in Iran. The complex project was called Operation *Sterkh*, which is Russian for Operation Siberian Crane.

It was a frustrating mission from the beginning. To collect and transport the eggs would demand much

*Vladimir Flint makes his way across the remote plains of eastern Siberia.*

31

patience, time, money and especially, hard work. Letters and telegrams flew back and forth between the two superpowers. Visits and meetings were arranged. Some government officials were very suspicious of the project. During George's first trip to the Soviet Union, he was harshly questioned by a man with a tape recorder. "Are you a Democrat or a Republican? Is the United States responsive enough to Brezhnev [the Soviet leader]?" More and more questions followed. But George was not afraid. Finally he said firmly, "I'm not a political person. I'm here as a scientist and a friend." He refused to say another word.

Officials in both countries were afraid of sending bird diseases back and forth across the continents. But George, Ron, and Vladimir presented a well thought-out plan to the U.S. Fish and Wildlife Service and to the Soviet Ministry of Agriculture, and obtained permits. The project moved along.

Yet the most important challenges still remained: to find fertile eggs at exactly the right time in Siberia and then fly them to their destination in Wisconsin. For the egg hatching to be successful, the eggs had to be taken from the nest between the 21st and the 25th days of the nesting period. If the scientists took the eggs away too early, the chicks inside might not survive the two-day air flight. If the nests were approached too late, the eggs might already have hatched. They also might hatch during the long plane trip. Ideally, the tiny chicks inside the eggs should be able to rest after the trip before they begin to hatch. To free itself of the eggshell takes a great deal of energy and effort for a tiny, weak chick.

Many unusual items and hardworking people were needed to complete this expensive and complicated task. Dr. Flint listed some of the necessities in his journal:

- good weather to allow the Soviets to survey the tundra for nests.
- 1 helicopter to land at the nests.
- 1 woolen sock to protect the egg during transport from nest to helicopter.
- 1 egg transport box.
- 1 hot-water bottle for heat.
- foam rubber and Styrofoam for insulation.
- 1 person to check the temperature in the box and turn the eggs every few hours.
- several jet airplanes to carry the eggs from the tundra to Wisconsin.

The obstacles seemed almost impossible to overcome. To transport fragile eggs safely and quickly three-quarters of the way around the world was a huge task.

*An aerial view of the vast and lonely tundra—breeding grounds of the Siberian crane*

CHAPTER 5

# RUSSIAN EGGS IN AMERICA

The tundra consists of thousands of square miles of wet, grassy marshland. From an airplane, there seems to be no land at all. It looks like thousands of lakes flowing together, forming a huge mirror. To see a single nest from the air is extremely difficult.

In earlier years Siberian crane nests had been found near the town of Chokurdakh in northern Yakutia, Siberia. This area could be reached only by helicopter or horse. Many of the Yakut people believed that if someone harmed the nest of a bird, bad luck would come. One of Vladimir Flint's most difficult jobs was to help the Yakuts understand why the scientists needed to take the crane eggs from the nests. Letters and calls from "heavy people" (officials in Moscow) helped. So did a film about saving Siberian cranes that George and Vladimir had made together. Finally, government officials gave permission for the egg pickup.

Vladimir Flint sent a famous photographer, Edward Nazarov, to the tundra to find a pair of Siberian cranes that he had photographed earlier. After much searching, Edward finally spotted the pair and a nest. He telegrammed

Vladimir, asking him to join him. Edward remained patiently hidden in a small, cramped grass hut near the birds until June 15, 1977, when Vladimir and his assistant, Sasha Sorokin, arrived. The eggs seemed healthy and were about ten days old.

All three men then left the nest and for the next five days flew for six or seven hours each day over the tundra. They needed to locate several crane nests so that there would be other choices in case something went wrong with the eggs they had already found. June 30, the final day for collecting, came closer. Searching for nests from the helicopter was extremely tiring on their eyes. When they did find a nest, it was important not to scare the cranes away from it, so the men would land about half a mile away. Quietly, they would hike from the helicopter to the nest. Tramping through marshes was slow and exhausting. Their feet sank as mud oozed around their boots. It took great effort to pull their feet out. More help was needed, so on June 21 six more workers arrived. At that point, Edward returned to the first nest in order to keep an eye on it. Meanwhile, preparations were made to gather the eggs on June 29 and 30.

Ice-covered lakes reflected bright sunshine. Spring was in full bloom. The air was filled with the cries and songs of many birds as well as the constant humming of

*Spotting a single nest from the air was one of the most difficult tasks of Operation Siberian Crane.*

millions of mosquitoes. Everyone was ready, but they were uneasy. The tundra is unpredictable; the weather can change suddenly. Then, on June 28, the wind shifted. Fog rolled in, and with it came rain and cold Arctic air. The airport closed because weather conditions made flying hazardous. Everyone's spirits fell. All the planning, calls, telegrams, meetings, visits, and money would be wasted.

On June 30 the evening sky finally brightened a bit; the dawn of July 1 was bright and warm. It was one day past the collection date. "Maybe they can still make it in time," said Vladimir.

The helicopter took off to collect Edward and the eggs. Vladimir found him standing beside an empty nest. The chicks had already hatched and left. Quickly the scientists got into the helicopter and began searching for the other nests that they had located earlier. All of these nests were also empty, but the scientists decided to keep looking as long as there was fuel left in their helicopter.

Finally they spotted another nest. They landed the helicopter. Edward, Sasha, and Vladimir excitedly ran through the cold, muddy water and knee-high grasses. Piled above the waterline, in a mound of yellow grasses, was one egg. The frightened parent birds were hiding in the nearby marshes. Gathering the precious egg, Vladimir slipped it carefully into a thick woolen sock. A feeble chirp came from near the nest. As the men looked toward the sound, they saw a ball of orange-yellow fluff drying in the sun—a baby crane. As the helicopter took off, the scientists watched the parent birds return to their chick.

After a few more hours, two more nests were located; two eggs were in each. Because they were almost out of fuel, the group decided to take all four eggs. It would be their last chance that year to try to begin the project to save the endangered Sibes. The precious cargo was flown by helicopter to the town of Chokurdakh. There, Vladimir Flint boarded an airplane and flew west to Moscow with the five eggs. Libby Anderson from ICF was waiting at the Sheremetyevo International Airport in Moscow.

In 1977, the relationship between the Soviet Union and the United States was very tense. Yet at that moment, an amazing act of simple cooperation took place. A large Russian man handed a rough plywood box to a slim young American woman. Inside were four eggs in four Russian socks. (One egg had already started to hatch, but the chick had died on the way to Moscow.) A hot-water bottle and layers of foam rubber and Styrofoam surrounded the socks to keep them warm.

Libby inspected the eggs. A decaying egg could explode and send out poisonous gases that could kill the other eggs. Everything smelled all right to her. She carefully turned the eggs 180°. If she did not turn them, part of the chicks inside might become attached to the shells.

Then Libby tried to board the plane, but a Soviet stewardess stopped her. "That box is too large to be in the plane with you," she said. "It will have to be stored in the hold of the airplane." Patiently Vladimir Flint explained that the crane eggs had to be watched and their temperature checked. Libby was finally given permission to board the plane with the box. She set her alarm clock. Every hour she

*The specially prepared box in which the Siberian crane eggs traveled from Yakutia to Wisconsin in 1977.*

opened the lid of the box to put lukewarm water in the hot-water bottle.

In London Libby had to change planes. Another stewardess told her again that the box of eggs was too big. Libby got so frustrated that she threatened to take the eggs out of the box and carry them inside her blouse. The threat worked! The amazed stewardess gave her permission to board.

After traveling 46 hours and 14,000 miles from Siberia, the eggs finally arrived at the Chicago airport. They were taken from their box by an agricultural inspector, who checked them to see if they looked healthy.

Then they were placed in a sealed container. Tired, Libby drove with them to the Biotron laboratory at the University of Wisconsin in Madison. Here special environmental studies of all kinds were conducted. In the laboratory George Archibald and his co-worker, Bill Gause, were anxiously waiting for the precious shipment. Very carefully, they and Libby placed the eggs in an incubator.

The next morning, July 3, was the big test—to see if the chicks inside the eggs were still alive. The eggs were gently lowered into lukewarm water. If the chicks were living, the eggs would bob high in the water with the pointed ends down. If the eggs were infertile or the chick inside was dead, they would float low in the water—motionless.

The two larger and darker eggs were lowered into the water first. They lay still and sank low. George shook them. He heard the sound of liquid inside. These eggs would never hatch. But the other two eggs bounced high in the water. These chicks were alive!

Now it was George and Bill's turn to act as "mother" to the two Siberian hopefuls. A computer maintained the temperature of the room at 99.75°F. Every few hours

George and Bill turned the eggs halfway around, just as the parent birds would have done. Days passed. George became anxious. He knew from field studies that normally the eggs of the wild cranes in Siberia would all have hatched by this time. Perhaps the tiny chicks had been weakened by the long journey and would silently die inside the eggs. Every few hours he checked for movement, but saw no signs of life.

On July 8, George and Bill decided to ease their tension by going to a movie. Finally, at midnight, they returned to the laboratory. One chick had made the first tiny hole in the egg! They heard peeping sounds and the wonderful rustling and crackling noises that come before the actual hatching process. "It was one of the most exciting moments of my life," George later recalled.

The eggs were moved from the incubator to the hatcher. The temperature was lowered 1°F and the humidity was increased. After nearly 41 hours of struggling, Vladimir (named after Dr. Flint) hatched on July 10. Kyta (the Yakut word for crane) hatched on July 12.

Soon after hatching, Vladimir was dry and fluffy. The little 4½-inch chick begged for food and ran around his carpeted pen. But little Kyta had a deformed leg that stuck out from her body. By tying the chick's feet together, George was able to gently pull her leg into its proper position. This treatment upset Kyta, however, who could

*Vladimir, after nearly 41 hours of struggling, hatches—and Operation Siberian Crane gets off to a successful start.*

have easily flipped on her back and died. She was placed on some soft cloth and either George or Bill stayed with her constantly to give her food and water. They kept her body upright and helped her walk. After three days, the chick was able to walk without support.

Three weeks after hatching, the two healthy Siberian crane chicks were driven from Madison to Baraboo to their new home at the International Crane Foundation.

Meanwhile, in Moscow, Dr. Flint had been despairing. Two weeks had gone by since the eggs had left him. Then a telegram arrived. With shaking hands Vladimir Flint opened the envelope. "The words jumped out at me as I read, 'Two eggs infertile; two chicks hatched and well. Congratulations. ICF.'"

Like George Archibald, Vladimir Flint said, "It was one of the greatest moments of my life."

# CHAPTER 6

# AEROFLOT AND FRIENDS

**M**arch 1978. The International Crane Foundation now had five healthy Siberian cranes: old Wolf from Germany; younger Hirakawa from Japan; the youngsters from the Soviet Union, Vladimir and Kyta; and Till, a newly imported male from Vogelpark Walsrode in West Germany. However, this group was not large enough to make a breeding program work. George, Ron, and Vladimir decided that the Soviets should once again return to the tundra and send another batch of eggs to Wisconsin.

The second egg transfer would be easier. The scientists had learned so much from the first trip. A smaller, more lightweight egg suitcase was constructed. Electric cables inside the case helped to maintain the correct temperature. Everything seemed ready when, suddenly, disaster struck in a new form.

A rare herpes virus attacked the cranes at ICF. One by one the great birds became sick and died. Different kinds of medicines were tried. Fast, frightening trips with feathered carcasses in the backseat of the car became common as workers hurried to the National Wildlife Health Center in Madison. The sickness seemed to be spreading among young birds who lived close together. In only two weeks, 22 precious cranes died.

Fortunately, the five Siberian cranes survived. ICF workers learned some important lessons. Now they would keep fewer birds in a flock, and they would move flocks onto new ground every year.

As June approached, Vladimir Flint could have decided not to send any more eggs to ICF because so many cranes had just died. However, he and his co-workers believed in their American friends. "We trusted George's authority and experience here," said Vladimir.

Now it was Ron Sauey's turn to make the egg pickup. In Moscow, Ron was to meet Vladimir Flint and the suitcase of eggs. When Ron saw the familiar cap and the dark gray suitcase in the airport, he decided to play a little joke. Ron walked up behind Vladimir and suddenly grabbed him by the shoulder. "What do you have in that suitcase?" he asked, seriously and authoritatively.

For a moment Vladimir hesitated, uncertain who was speaking. Then he turned, saw Ron's face, and grinned. The two men hugged in a warm Russian-style greeting.

As they drove to the international airport, Vladimir told Ron that he had found seven eggs this time. The two men stopped en route to look at the eggs and to take pictures of them. A loud peeping came from the open suitcase.

"This one is hatching!" said Ron.

"No, it's just talking to us," said Vladimir hopefully.

However, as he turned the egg, they both saw a small hole on its side. Whistling between his teeth, Vladimir closed the suitcase carefully. "I hope this chick can survive the 20-hour trip to the United States."

Ron sat in Aeroflot (the Soviet airline) Flight 315 to New York City with the suitcase on his knees. Small cheeping noises were coming out of it. Many of the passengers on the plane were curious. Ron explained Operation *Sterkh* to them. For 13 hours Ron watched over the suitcase, juggling it every hour to keep each egg evenly warm.

By the time the plane reached New York, the hatching egg was still alive. The chick was beginning to turn inside its shell. It was not going to wait for a nice warm incubator!

Unfortunately, Ron had only 10 minutes to get to the plane that would take him to Chicago. "You'll never make it," said the official from the Department of Agriculture. "It'll take 30 minutes to get to the right terminal!"

"I've got to," yelled Ron as he ran out of the office. It was Fourth of July weekend; all the other flights were filled.

The agricultural agent took pity on Ron. Grabbing his arm, he took him to his own parked car outside the terminal near the runway. "We don't have time to take the usual roads," shouted the agent above the noise of the huge planes. "We're going to have to take a more interesting route."

Soon Ron and the agent were speeding down the runways, dodging enormous Boeing 747 planes that were taxiing alongside them. In no time they crossed the airport and Ron was allowed through a door that is normally locked.

"Hey, where do you think you're going?" shouted a police guard. Ron kept running. The last sounds he heard were the voices of the agricultural agent arguing with the policeman. Ron made it to the gate, holding his suitcase as if it were a box of jewels. He was the last passenger to board the jumbo DC-10 jet to Chicago.

When Ron finally reached the laboratory in Madison, Wisconsin, he anxiously opened the suitcase. There, looking wet but healthy, was a downy Siberian chick sitting on a sweater that had been lent to Ron. Everyone decided to call this chick Aeroflot because it was the first chick to have hatched on an airplane at 30,000 feet.

Four of the other six eggs hatched, but one chick died a few days later. Now there were four new, beautiful Siberian crane chicks at the International Crane Foundation—Aeroflot, Bazov, Edward, and Tanya—to join the five older Sibes.

*Aeroflot—he couldn't wait for the incubator.*

CHAPTER 7

# A NEW HOME
# IN RUSSIA

Although the first steps of the captive breeding program at ICF seemed to be working, the numbers of wild Siberian cranes were still decreasing. Later in 1978, Vladimir Flint decided to visit ICF to learn more about the captive management of the endangered cranes. There he watched his young namesake, Vladimir, and Kyta settled in pens on the green hills of Baraboo. "Of course, my godchildren did not greet me very warmly," he said afterward. "They didn't even recognize me!"

Flint's visit convinced him that the Soviet Union should have a breeding center like the one at ICF. After he eagerly discussed the idea with other Soviet scientists, a beautiful forest and marshland 174 miles southeast of Moscow on the Pra River was chosen. Called the Oka Nature Reserve, the area was already home to 50 kinds of mammals and about 200 kinds of birds. And most amazingly, about 35 pairs of nesting Eurasian cranes lived within the boundaries of Oka.

To begin the center, in June 1979 Vladimir Flint and Sasha Sorokin brought four eggs from Yakutia. Before they could get them to Oka, one of the eggs began to hatch on the plane to Moscow. Acting quickly, they brought the egg to Vladimir's Moscow apartment and placed it on a hot-water bottle. For many long hours that night, they watched the wet chick struggle to break through its shell.

They debated whether to help it. Helping a chick too soon often results in its bleeding to death. Yet failing to help a weak chick can also cause its death. Finally, Vladimir announced to Sasha that he was going to pull the chick from the egg. Sasha objected and ran into another room. Fortunately, the fragile blood vessels that connect the chick to the shell had closed. Vladimir's risky operation was a success. George (named after George Archibald) was born.

George and the three eggs were taken to the Oka crane center, where the eggs hatched in a new electric incubator that had been sent there by ICF. At first the four young Siberian cranes were healthy and grew rapidly. However, after about six weeks, the three incubator-hatched cranes weakened and died. Only George lived.

That summer, George Archibald visited Oka and met his namesake. He and Vladimir discussed the reasons for the deaths of the birds. They decided the cranes' diets had not included everything they needed to be healthy. Somehow, young George had been strong enough to survive despite an imbalanced diet. A year later, George

Archibald asked the director of the West German bird park, Vogelpark Walsrode, to give fresh crane pellets to the Soviets. In exchange, the scientists at Oka sent some Siberian crane eggs and stork chicks to West Germany.

For the next six years, the Soviets would hatch and raise 18 Siberian cranes. Each year George Archibald would faithfully visit Oka, cooperating with the Soviet scientists in their efforts.

At both Oka and ICF, Soviet and American scientists were trying not only to breed captive cranes, but also to learn more about the mysteries of the wild Siberian cranes.

While they knew that western Sibes wintered in India and Iran, they still did not know where they bred in Russia. An unexpected discovery helped solve this problem.

In June 1978, some Soviet tourists had been canoeing down a branch of the Ob River just east of the Ural Mountains in western Siberia. On a sandbar they found a young wild crane chick that could not yet fly. They took the cute bird with them for a long distance, but they knew they could not keep it. When they reached the town of Gorki, they asked if there was someone there who would care for the bird. An animal lover, Tamara Soldatova, accepted the young crane.

Under her loving care it grew so tall and strong that she could no longer keep it in her house. It began a strange outdoor life, living beneath her house in the company of a chained fox and several husky sled dogs. Fed plenty of fish, the hardy bird flourished. Finally it grew so large that Mrs. Soldatova wrote a letter to the local newspaper to see if someone who knew more about cranes than she did would be interested in her bird.

Luckily, the letter was forwarded to the University of Moscow, where Vladimir Flint heard about it. Excitedly, he asked Sasha Sorokin to try to find the crane. It was snowing when Sasha got off the plane in the town of Gorki. There to meet him was one of the villagers, the crane's head bulging from beneath his coat. Sasha yelled with joy. He recognized that the crane was an endangered young Sibe. He brought it back to Vladimir's Moscow apartment, where the ornithologists gave the dirty, smelly bird three warm baths with baby soap. His feathers had been stained yellow-brown, and he smelled terribly of rotten fish. However, the crane stood quietly in the middle of the room. He could be picked up and put down without protest. He was tame. Vladimir was so delighted with him that he named the bird Sauey, after his friend Ron Sauey at ICF. Moscow apartments are not healthy places for cranes that pick at shiny objects, so Sauey was taken to live at the new Oka breeding center.

The finding of Sauey was a wonderful clue to the exact location of the breeding grounds of the western population of wild Siberian cranes. The only way for a young chick to

be near the Ob River was to have been born there, because he was too young to be able to fly.

In the summer of 1981 Sasha went to western Siberia to look for crane nests. He flew low, back and forth over the area where the tourists had found Sauey. Later that autumn, George Archibald excitedly opened a letter from Vladimir. It read:

> We have good news. Sasha Sorokin has found Siberian cranes in the lower Ob region. He discovered eight breeding pairs on the River Kunovat, not far from where Sauey was found. Sasha brought three eggs back with him. Now we have another chick from the western flock. His name is Julius.

Sauey and Julius were very important chicks. If this western flock were killed during their wintering periods in Iran, Afghanistan, or India, Sauey and Julius alone would have the special genes of that wild population.

*Sauey, the tame Sibe, inspects Vladimir Flint's Moscow apartment.*

*Sibes in flight—the birds migrate long distances over the same routes year after year.*

# CHAPTER 8

# MIGRATING THROUGH AFGHANISTAN AND PAKISTAN

**R**aising an endangered species in captivity cannot save it from extinction. While scientists were working at Oka and at ICF, they were also cooperating in projects to save the Siberian cranes in the wild. On the faraway, cold marshes of the Arctic Siberian tundra, the breeding wild Siberian cranes have few enemies and plenty of food. Danger comes when they leave the tundra, migrating south to their warm wintering grounds.

In mid- to late September, the cranes leave with their chicks to find shallow-water feeding areas free of ice and snow. The migration of the great white birds begins at dawn. The birds move restlessly and noisily until suddenly a few families or small groups begin to "flap-fly" away.

They gracefully soar upward on warm, rising air currents called thermals. Once they have gained altitudes between 6,000 and 15,000 feet, they stop flapping. Now they glide along, descending very slightly, for great distances. This kind of flying uses much less energy than flying by flapping the wings. When the cranes meet another rising air current, they again soar up with it. All the while they are calling and calling. Since they often fly more than a mile high, they are usually unseen as they sail to their destination. Only their beautiful voices float downward.

The Siberian crane makes one of the longest migrations known for a large bird, at least 5,000 miles on its western route. Cranes learn their routes when they are very young. They use the same routes over and over, year after year, flying over Arctic tundra, leafy forests, sand deserts, and tropical scrub.

Dangers exist everywhere along this journey. Sometimes violent storms send young birds off course. Or the wetlands where they rest and feed along the route may have disappeared. Then the cranes cannot find the right kind of food. Often the wetlands have been polluted by chemicals and pesticides and the water makes the cranes sick.

Many cranes are killed by sport hunters. For the cranes that migrate south from western Siberia, these hunters wait on dark, moonless nights in the mountain passes of the Hindu Kush Mountains of Afghanistan and Pakistan. Tame cranes are placed as decoys along the migration route. When migrating birds flying overhead hear the cries of the captive cranes, they fly lower to investigate. Then the hunters, hidden in trenches near the decoys, stand up and throw a special weapon made of three ropes with metal weights attached to the ends. The ropes tangle around the legs of the flying birds and pull them to the ground. In 1982, about 1,500 cranes of various species were caught in this way. Some were eaten and some were kept as pets or "watchdogs." Rare Siberian cranes have been seen hanging dead in a meat market in Kabul, the capital of Afghanistan.

Dangers exist all along the cranes' migration route. Perhaps the most disturbing is the threat posed by hunters in the mountains of Afghanistan. Here, in a Kabul market, a Eurasian crane is being sold for its meat.

Since 1979, Afghanistan has suffered terribly from the effects of civil war. Hungry, desperate people and migrating cranes do not successfully exist together. Even Vladimir Flint, who has spent years trying to save the endangered birds, sadly admits, "If I were hungry, I'd eat the last crane, too."

In Afghanistan and Pakistan, the sport of capturing live cranes has become more and more popular. Wealthy villagers will pay large sums for a pair trained to unison call. Alarmed by these reports, Ron and George encouraged a young ICF worker and educator, Steven Landfried, to help in Pakistan. He created a questionnaire for hunters so he could learn more about them. He found out that the sport hunters themselves knew that there were fewer and fewer cranes, but they liked to "act like men," to practice with their ropes and to kill and capture animals.

Steve worked hard to educate the hunters, as well as Pakistani officials. Now, because of his efforts, the capturing and shooting of Siberian cranes are illegal acts in Pakistan. Even selling the cranes is against the law, partly as a result of Steve's work. He made a slide show to help hunters tell a Siberian crane from other kinds of cranes. There are big fines for hunting other crane species as well. The radio station broadcasts educational programs about crane conservation. The government issued a postage stamp featuring Siberian cranes. Best of all, the Pakistan

On the stamp: साइबेरियाई सारस SIBERIAN CRANE — भारत INDIA 2⁸⁵

*ICF is working hard to protect the crane by educating people and making them aware of its value. As part of this effort, the Indian and Pakistani governments issued postage stamps featuring Siberian cranes.*

Wildlife Department will pay hunters who bring in wild, healthy cranes. Officials then put leg bands on the cranes and release them.

The Pakistani government is also trying to encourage villagers who have captive cranes to breed them and release the young into the wild. That way, they can add to the small population of cranes who migrate through Pakistan on their way to India.

# CHAPTER 9

# WINTERING IN
# INDIA AND IRAN

Siberian cranes once spent their winters along the south-eastern shore of the Caspian Sea in Iran as well as in the wetlands of northern India. But Iranian hunters liked the sweet-tasting meat of this huge bird. Hunters killed so many Sibes that by the 1970s, none of this species had been seen in Iran for a long time. So for many years the only known wintering place where wild Siberian cranes could easily be studied was in India.

Every year, cranes from western Siberia arrive at the Keoladeo Ghana Bird Sanctuary in Bharatpur sometime between November and January. During the early 1970s, when Ron Sauey was studying the cranes, there were as many as 72 Sibes there. However, fewer birds returned each winter. In 1979, Ron and George received a desperate letter from Raj Singh, an Indian ornithologist. Only 12 Siberian cranes had come back to the beautiful sanctuary that year. Extinction seemed very close.

Though Keoladeo was a state nature reserve, the local government did not enforce the laws protecting the safety of the endangered Siberian cranes. Hunters stalked the waterfowl. People from nearby villages stripped the land of wood for fuel. Up to 10,000 water buffalo and cattle grazed daily inside the reserve. Carts, cars, scooters, and tour buses frightened the birds. Troubled, Ron returned to India and recorded the anxious behavior of the disturbed Siberian cranes. He noted the interrupted eating, intense staring, and frightened purring of the uneasy birds.

Ron gently talked about his concerns to everyone he met—forest guards, village people, and government workers. He even wrote to the Indian Prime Minister, Indira Gandhi. The hard work of Ron and other concerned people bore fruit. In April 1981, the Keoladeo reserve was declared a national park of India. A high wall was built around the area. No longer could local people graze their herds, cut firewood, or hunt in Keoladeo.

Angry and frustrated, villagers rioted at the gate of the new park. They threw rocks at the police, who then opened fire. Seven Indian citizens were killed. Many more were wounded. As a result of the riot, the government decided to give the villagers food for their cattle and money to buy fuel. This sad drama shows the great pressure on the few remaining wetlands in India and other nations where people and wildlife compete for the same resources.

In 1983 Bharatpur was the scene of a happier event. The International Crane Foundation and the government of India hosted the first International Crane Workshop. For the first time crane researchers from China, India, Iran,

*As more and more people take over the earth's wetlands, fewer and fewer habitats remain for wildlife.*

Pakistan, the Soviet Union, and the United States came together to share information and plan for future projects to help the endangered Siberian cranes.

In 1989 a second international meeting, the Asian Congress, was organized by Jim Harris, deputy director of ICF. Scientists from six countries came to India to voice once more their deep concern about the nearly extinct

Siberian cranes wintering in India. Only 17 of these wild birds came to Keoladeo during the winter of 1989-1990, because the water levels in the park were too low. In reaction to the concern of the scientists, the Indian government agreed to provide more water by digging wells and canals. In exchange, Vladimir Flint said the Soviet Union would give the Indian government some young Siberian cranes from the eastern flock. Once more, people from diverse nations were able to work together on behalf of the endangered Sibes.

Meanwhile, there was hopeful news from Iran. Back in 1978 a scientist had spotted nine Siberian cranes near a town at the southern end of the Caspian Sea. No Sibes had been seen near the Caspian Sea for the last hundred years.

George Archibald went to Iran to investigate and discovered that a group of Sibes was wintering right in the middle of a duck-hunting area. George knew the cranes were in danger, but he could do nothing to protect them. For three years after he left Iran, George heard nothing more about the cranes. Then in 1982 a letter came from a Finnish woman, Ellen Tavokoli, who lived in the area where the cranes had been seen. Amazingly, 11 cranes remained.

Every year the Finnish woman observed the cranes. In 1990 she wrote that 12 Siberian cranes were still wintering in Iran. They had somehow survived despite the hunters.

Today, scientists are still trying to learn exactly when

the cranes fly and where they rest. If they can discover the 5,000-mile migration route from western Siberia to Iran and India, they will have a much better chance of protecting the cranes en route. They have developed a special satellite tracker that will help locate birds as they migrate. Before using the new system on Siberian cranes, the scientists tested it on another crane species. They fitted a Eurasian crane named Katya with one. In 1990, they tracked her from Siberia to her winter home in Iran. The techniques the researchers learned from her journey will, they hope, help save the much rarer Siberian crane.

CHAPTER 10

# WONDERFUL NEWS
# IN CHINA

China is home to seven of the world's fifteen crane species. It is also a vital link in saving the eastern Siberian crane population. Although no one knew exactly where, the eastern Sibes wintered somewhere in warm southern China, along the great Yangtze River. But for a long time, neither American nor Russian scientists were allowed into China to investigate.

Even Chinese scientists couldn't help. During Mao Zedong's Cultural Revolution in the late 1960s, many birds and animals were listed as pests and therefore killed. Vast areas of wetlands, homes to thousands of birds and animals, were drained to make agricultural fields. Even the most famous Chinese ornithologists were forced to work on farms and in factories, and the study of wildlife at universities became the source of jokes. No research on wild birds was pursued at all. Letters sent by ICF to Chinese scientists were seldom answered.

Fortunately, great changes occurred when Mao died and new Communist officials came to power. In 1977 the Chinese researchers were able to return to work. The Ministry of Forestry established more nature reserves, including one at Zhalong, in northeastern China, in 1979. Zhalong is a huge marshland, a green waving ocean of reeds with dots of lakes in between. It acts as a funnel for migrating birds that want to avoid flying over the Gobi Desert. Red-crowned cranes, white-napped cranes, eastern white storks, purple herons, white spoonbills, and black-headed ibis can all be found there at some point during the year. In the reserve one can hear a symphony of sounds: the repeated choruses of hovering skylarks, the melodies of black-browed warblers, the low voices of gigantic bitterns, and, in the distance, the calls of red-crowned cranes. In April and May it is a rest stop for the Sibes as they travel north to their Yakut breeding grounds from their winter homes somewhere in southern China.

In 1979, George Archibald wrote to China's most famous ornithologist, Professor Cheng Tsohsin, telling him that he would be working in the neighboring countries of Russia and Japan. Some months later, George received the long-awaited invitation to visit the Institute of Zoology in Beijing, the capital of China. While there, George made friends with Cheng and with Zhou Fuchang and Deng Wenning, two Siberian crane researchers who had been searching unsuccessfully for the birds' wintering grounds in China.

There was little money for this project. Zhou and Deng sent questionnaires to people all over southern China.

Every answer was investigated, which meant that the two men had to take a bus to some remote place, only to discover that the sighting was a white egret or a white stork. Then, during the winter of 1980-1981, another huge piece of the crane puzzle fell into place. They discovered a hundred Siberian cranes feeding in the wetlands at Lake P'o-yang Hu in Jiangxi province. They had found the wintering grounds of the eastern Sibes.

Lake P'o-yang Hu is China's largest lake, a place where the water seems to touch the sky. The Yangtze River crosses the north end. Each spring and summer flood-waters from the great river and five other smaller rivers fill the lake. In winter the lake shrinks to one-fifth of its summer size and is surrounded by wide expanses of grasslands and mud flats. The Siberian cranes stay in the shallows bordering the winter lakes. As these lakes get smaller, the cranes follow the retreating edges, digging up plant tubers, clams, and snails. "It was wonderful to see flocks of one hundred or more snowy white cranes circling and banking, their black-tipped wings against the azure-blue sky," said Zhou.

When the cranes were discovered that first winter, the local people were shooting birds, including Sibes, with cannons mounted on small, flat-bottomed boats. The hunters dressed in white costumes, letting the wind blow their boats soundlessly across the water near the feeding birds.

Once they opened fire, dead cranes and other birds lay all over the ground.

Fortunately, the Ministry of Forestry soon protected the Lake P'o-yang area by creating a nature reserve in the main wetlands. The hunters' guns were silenced.

In the years to come, ICF scientists and their Chinese friends carefully counted the endangered birds. From 1981 to 1984, the Siberian crane population dramatically increased from 100 to 400, then from 800 to 1,350. In 1992, it was estimated that approximately 2,600 cranes of the eastern Siberian flock wintered in China. This was hopeful news indeed.

The number of Siberian cranes increased not only because the wetlands were protected, but also because the people living near the cranes' wintering grounds began to be educated. Scientists give slide shows and distribute colorful photographs of the great white birds to the Chinese people. In addition, the people are taught how to make better farms without draining so many wetlands. Tourists are encouraged to come to see the wildlife, which brings money to the area.

The beautiful white cranes from eastern Siberia will continue to be secure at Lake P'o-yang Hu in south China as long as the lake and the government protection remain. However, a dam proposed for the Yangtze River upstream from P'o-yang would block much of the spring floodwater.

Then the wild celery might not grow and the Sibes might not find their winter food—the celery tubers that flourish in this vast wetland. And the largest remaining flock of Sibes in the world would again be in danger of extinction.

CHAPTER 11

# AMERICAN AND SOVIET OFFSPRING

As Ron, George, Vladimir, and all their co-workers in many countries worked to establish reserves, better laws, and more education programs to help the remaining wild Siberian cranes, exciting work continued to be done with raising captive cranes at Oka and ICF. At first there were many setbacks. In 1980 at ICF, Hirakawa, the Siberian crane from Japan, was mated to Till from West Germany. Hirakawa laid ten eggs; four of them were fertile. Sadly, however, each chick died in the incubator during the hatching process.

Frustrated, the staff at ICF decided to try a new hatching method. They thought that a living bird might be better to use than an incubator. A living bird is more sensitive to the needs of the chick inside the egg than an incubator. So they obtained four breeding pairs of a different kind of crane, the Florida sandhill crane. In 1981 Hirakawa laid ten more eggs. Those eggs were put into the nests of the sandhills. Three of the eggs were fertile. One tiny chick died inside the egg; another hatched but died from an infection of the intestines. But egg number seven lived! Dushenka was born. The Russian name means "little loved one."

*A closeup of a captive Sibe—raising and breeding cranes is a difficult job, one that takes hard work and ingenuity.*

73

The wonderful news of this event spread quickly. Reporters called to ask questions about this special chick. Soon Dushenka was known as the "peep heard round the world"—the first Siberian crane to be born in captivity from captive parents. If all went well, she would be successfully paired with one of the young cranes from Yakutia. Their offspring would represent hope for all the Siberian cranes of the earth...a symbol of the friendship between once-hostile nations and of renewal for one of the most endangered species in the world.

Dushenka's young wild-born Siberian crane cousins were also thriving at ICF—Aeroflot, Edward, Bazov, Kyta, Tanya, and Vladimira. (It was discovered that Vladimir was a female crane! Vladimir Flint laughingly says, "All the chicks named after me were girls!") Seventeen other young Sibes also flourished at Oka reserve in Russia.

In spite of all the good news, the ICF staff was concerned that the young wild Siberian cranes brought as eggs from Yakutia by Libby and Ron were not laying eggs. It seemed strange, because other kinds of cranes raised in captivity were breeding at three or four years of age.

Finally, in 1984, Vladimira and Bazov, a young Siberian male, were ready. One spring morning, Vladimira stood protectively near her first egg. It was promptly placed into the nest of two breeding sandhill cranes. The chick that hatched from Vladimira's egg was important. Named Dr.

*Two-day-old Dushenka, the "peep heard round the world"*

Sahib, she was the first captive Siberian chick born of parents imported as eggs.

During the late 1980s relations between the United States and the Soviet Union became much friendlier. With the breakup of the Soviet Union and the collapse of communism in 1991, the last official barriers between the two countries broke down. Now it is easier to exchange information and scientific visits. Phone calls can be made; faxes fly between the United States and Russia. However, because of the severe economic problems in Russia today, fewer and fewer funds are available to protect wildlife.

As time goes by, Vladimir and George and their co-workers are learning more about how to raise captive Siberian cranes successfully. George is studying crane diets in western Siberia. In Wisconsin, crane puppets help young chicks learn how to eat. ICF workers dress up in large crane costumes when they take young chicks out for walks. Scientists hope the Sibes will learn to follow cranes, not people. Researchers have now discovered that crane chicks raised by a different crane species will not form pairs with their own kind. It is important that they establish normal relationships with their relatives in the wild . . . because that is where the future of the Siberian crane lies.

CHAPTER 12

# SYMBOLS OF HOPE

The story of the Siberian crane is a tale of both deep despair and—so far—great hope. Since the international effort to save the crane was launched, great gains in conservation have been made. Yet the danger of extinction remains. Wetlands, so necessary to the birds' survival, are threatened the world over. The human population continues to explode, squeezing all wildlife into smaller and smaller pockets of land. Because the Siberian cranes themselves gather in groups, large numbers of cranes may be wiped out suddenly by fire, predators, disease, chemical wastes, or pesticides. No one will ever know when the last crane may be killed by a hunter's gun or a soldier's stray bullet.

Vladimir Flint feels that it is difficult to predict the successful end of Operation Siberian Crane. "When we once again see nesting pairs on the Oka mud flats, when breeding grounds are preserved, and cranes begin to winter regularly in increasing numbers in Iran and India, then we can stop worrying about the cranes."

The large numbers of eastern Siberian cranes, about 2,600 when this book was written, remains a cause for optimism. Yet the population of the western flocks has continued to plummet. In 1991, there were only 10 or 11 Sibes wintering in Iran, and only 6 in India, due in large part to the massacre of the cranes in the Hindu Kush Mountains.

In December 1991, crane specialists from the United States, Russia, Iran, India, and Pakistan met in Karachi, Pakistan, to discuss emergency measures to help save the western flock. Each country put forth its plan to promote conservation and education. The most dangerous place in the world for cranes remains war-torn Afghanistan, where hunting is uncontrolled. Yet even there, Steven Landfried, who did such valuable work in Pakistan, plans to develop an education program for people who live along the migration route. This program will coincide with the satellite tracking research that is being developed.

Tracking the cranes along the route may be the western Sibes' best chance of survival. In the summer of 1991, ICF researcher Mini Nagendran completed an important step in Operation Siberian Crane. She brought Siberian crane eggs from ICF in Wisconsin and from Vogelpark Walsrode in Germany to Russia. The eggs were brought over in an incubator to Gorki, the nearest place to the western breeding area that had electricity. The chicks hatched and three survived—Bugle, Vodka, and Walsrode. Mini brought them to the Siberian wilderness, where she reared them in the hope that they would join wild Siberian cranes on their migration to India or Iran.

Dressed in a crane costume and using taped crane sounds so that the youngsters would identify with cranes, not people, Mini trained the chicks. She taught them how to forage and protect themselves from bears, wolves, otters, eagles, and people. After three months, one youngster was fitted with a radio transmitter and then all three birds were released into the wild. Unfortunately, the wild crane family with which they were to fly south departed early, leaving the young cranes behind.

In 1992 with the help of the Russians, Mini is rearing other chicks and hopes to release them earlier in the breeding season. However, funds for this project are difficult to obtain because of Russia's economic problems.

Steven's and Mini's efforts are but two examples of the extraordinary efforts being made to preserve the western flock. Why go to such lengths to save the Sibes?

When Ron Sauey was carefully watching the Siberian crane eggs during the long flight from Moscow to Wisconsin in 1978, the woman who was sitting next to him asked, "Why do you want so much to save these birds?"

Ron answered, "Because they are so beautiful. Because I get excited when I see them. There is no reason for them to become extinct. Such thinking won't influence an economist or a general. But the birds are so beautiful. Why lose that?"

*An ICF worker trains chicks in Siberia for eventual release into the wild. The researcher wears a crane costume so that the young birds will identify with cranes, not people.*

The woman was so impressed with Ron's answer that she let him use her best sweater, a yellow cashmere, to keep the tiny, newly hatched chick warm.

The late American environmental author Rachel Carson would have had another reason for saving the Siberian crane. She would have felt that the leaving and return of the beautiful birds, year after year, is an event that people can count on. It is like the coming of dawn after night and the advent of spring after winter. Such repeated events give people a feeling of healing and well-being, and assure them of the continuation of life.

Sometimes there are very practical reasons for preserving animals and plants, fish, birds, or insects. In the past, amazing discoveries have been made. For example, the tiny common flower called a periwinkle has been used in the battle against leukemia, a cancer that affects children as well as adults. The bark of the Pacific yew tree has been found to help cure ovarian and breast cancers. We can never be sure what living things may help to save our own lives.

But most of all, cranes are symbols of peace and life in many countries all over the world. One story, from Japan, illustrates the profound influence they have on people.

Everything changed on August 6, 1945, for the people of the Japanese city of Hiroshima. That was the day the atom bomb was dropped. Sadako Sasaki was only a small girl when the "thunderbolt" turned Hiroshima into a desert. Yet 11 years later, she learned that she had the dreaded A-bomb disease caused by the radiation she absorbed when the bomb fell.

Sadako knew an old Japanese legend about cranes—graceful birds who live long, long lives. The legend said that if one makes a thousand paper cranes, strings them on a cord, and then hangs them in the temple as an offering, any prayer that one makes will be answered.

So Sadako began to fold paper cranes. After a few weeks she had folded over 300 cranes, and they hung from the ceiling in her hospital room. In spite of her headaches and dizzy spells, Sadako kept folding. She grew worse, and died soon after folding her 644th paper crane.

Her sad classmates finished folding the final 356 cranes. Sadako was buried with her 1,000 cranes. And then her friends and other children from all over Japan began to dream of building a special monument to all the children who had been killed by the atom bomb. Throughout Japan, young people collected money.

Now a statue of Sadako stands in the Hiroshima Peace Park. On top of a granite mountain she holds a golden crane in her outstretched hands. Every year, thousands of people place paper cranes at her feet on August 6, Peace Day. They say the prayer that is written at the base of the statue:

> This is our cry.
> This is our prayer.
> Peace in the world.

Though with the end of the cold war the threat of nuclear war has decreased, it has not disappeared. As long as countries disagree about territory, or trade, or politics, or religion, there will be war, and even nuclear war will remain a possibility. That is why friendship and cooperation between countries and populations will always be so important. The effort to save the Siberian crane forged such a friendship during the bleakest days of the cold war, and it remains a model for joint efforts to come. As Vladimir Flint has said, the crane project "showed us that people of different countries can work closely on good projects if they know each other as well as I know George Archibald and the guys from ICF. If you would ask me to name my five best friends in the whole world, George would be there."

For his part, George Archibald says, "I love the Russians very much. They are warm and very funny. Their appreciation, their reciprocity, has made it a great joy to work with them. If we had more of these kinds of exchanges, the world would be a little safer place."

Saving the magnificent Siberian crane will continue to require all the goodwill and ingenuity that the international scientific community can muster. On such cooperation does the future of the Siberian crane—and our own—depend.

## Note

In September 1983 George Archibald received the famous Order of the Golden Arc, the Netherlands' highest award for outstanding service to the conservation of wildlife. In May 1985 he was awarded the Gold Medal, the highest honor of the World Wildlife Fund.

Vladimir Flint also received the Order of the Golden

Arc for his work helping people understand that we belong to one world. In December 1987 Vladimir Flint received the prestigious Audubon Medal from the National Audubon Society of the United States. He was the first Soviet citizen to be so honored.

Sadly, Ron Sauey died in 1987. His work, however, lives on. His deep concern about the fate of the Siberian cranes may be one reason why this species is not yet extinct.

# Glossary

**adapt**—to adjust; to change in order to survive new conditions

**endangered species**—a kind of animal or plant in danger of becoming extinct, or dying off

**extinct**—no longer living anywhere on earth

**fertile egg**—an egg that has living young inside it

**gene**—one of the tiny units of a cell of an animal or plant that determines the characteristics that an offspring inherits from its parents

**habitat**—the area where an animal or plant naturally lives or grows

**herpes**—a disease often fatal to cranes, caused by a virus; it usually attacks the liver and spleen, is highly contagious, and is untreatable

**incubate**—to hatch eggs by keeping them warm

**ornithologist**—an expert in the study of birds and their habits

**ovarian cancer**—cancer of the female reproductive organs

**predator**—an animal that lives by capturing and feeding on other animals

**prey**—an animal hunted for food by another animal

**satellite tracker**—a man-made object that has been put into orbit around the earth in order to track the movements of cranes; it picks up radio signals from transmitters fitted on the birds and relays information about their positions to ground stations

**species**—a group of animals or plants that have certain characteristics in common; lions and tigers are two different species of cat

**tundra**—a vast, nearly flat, treeless plain in Arctic regions

**wetlands**—areas that contain much soil moisture; a swamp, marsh, or bog

# Chronology

**1965** Vladimir Flint finds Siberian crane eggs for his collection, thus discovering part of the vast breeding area in eastern Siberia.

**1972** Ron Sauey and George Archibald lease the Sauey farm in Baraboo, Wisconsin; the International Crane Foundation (ICF) is born.

**1972** U.S./USSR environmental agreement is signed, in spite of the cold war.

**1973** Ron begins fieldwork at the Siberian crane wintering grounds in Keoladeo Ghana Bird Sanctuary, in Bharatpur, India.

**1976** Philis and Wolf arrive at ICF from Philadelphia and West Germany.

**1976** The U.S. Fish and Wildlife Service and the Soviet Ministry of Agriculture sign an agreement to work on Siberian crane projects.

**1977** Operation Siberian Crane begins. The eggs flown from Yakutia (eastern Siberia) hatch at ICF; Vladimir and Kyta are the first Siberian cranes to hatch successfully in captivity.

**1978** Herpes virus strikes ICF.

**1978**  Ron Sauey brings seven eggs from the USSR. Aeroflot hatches en route. Later, Bazov, Edward, and Tanya are born.

**1978**  Crane breeding center begins at the Oka Nature Reserve in the USSR.

**1978**  A young Siberian crane chick is found near the Ob River in western Siberia.

**1978**  George goes to Iran and discovers a new population of Siberian cranes living in a duck-hunting area.

**1979**  George Archibald visits China at the invitation of its foremost ornithologist, Dr. Cheng Tsohsin.

**1979**  Only 12 Siberian cranes winter at Keoladeo Ghana Bird Sanctuary in India.

**1979**  Zhalong Natural Reserve is established in China.

**1981**  A hundred Siberian cranes are discovered wintering at Lake P'o-yang Hu in southern China.

**1981**  The breeding grounds of western Siberian cranes are located.

**1981**  Keoladeo is declared a national park by Indira Gandhi.

**1981** Dushenka is born at ICF, the first Siberian crane to be born in captivity from captive parents.

**1983** The first International Crane Workshop is held in Bharatpur, India.

**1984** Dr. Sahib is born, the first captive Siberian chick born of parents imported as eggs.

**1991** Twenty crane specialists from five nations meet in Karachi, Pakistan, to discuss efforts to save the last western flocks of the Siberian crane.

**1991** The current status of the last remaining Siberian cranes is:

> 2,600 winter at Lake P'o-yang Hu, China
> 11 winter in Iran
> 6 winter in India

# Bibliography

Anderson, Elizabeth. 1978. *Four Case Studies in US–USSR Wildlife Cooperation,* Project for degree, master of professional studies in agriculture, Cornell University.

Archibald, George. 1975. Crane Over Panmunjon: Manchurian Cranes. *International Wildlife,* September pp. 18–21.

——1981. Last Call for the Siberian Crane. *Natural History,* March, pp. 58–61.

Bauer, D. 1976. Promise in Dawn's Wake. *Sports Illustrated,* Feb. 16, p. 54ff.

Brolga Bugle. Fall 1974–February 1988. International Crane Foundation, Baraboo, WI.

Changing Faces of War. *Beyond War,* Issue 38, April 1988.

Crane Man. 1982. *New Yorker,* May 24, pp. 30–31.

Daniels, P. Ambassador of Cranes. *National Wildlife,* April/ May, 1983, pp. 33–37.

Flint, Vladimir E. 1980. *Operation Crane,* Moscow.

Graham, F., Jr. 1982. The Ancient Lineage. *Audubon,* July,1982.

Hare, J. D. 1985. Crane Cooperation: A Step toward World Peace. *National Wildlife,* Aug./Sept., p. 26.

Harris, James T. 1981. International Crane Foundation. *Blair and Ketcham,* Sept., pp. 62-67.

——1979. Detente for Cranes. *Animal Kingdom,* Dec./Jan., pp. 27-34.

Harrison, G. H. 1978. Crane Saviors of Baraboo. *Audubon,* March, pp. 25-28.

Hayashida, T. 1983. The Japanese Crane: Bird of Happiness. *National Geographic,* Oct., pp. 542-546.

Ingber, D. 1984. Odyssey of a Crane Lover. *Science Digest,* July, pp. 52-57ff.

Johnsgard, Paul A. 1983. *Cranes of the World,* Bloomington, IN.

Kraper, G. L., and J. Eldridge. 1984. Crane River. *Natural History,* Jan. pp. 68-75.

Madson, J. 1974. Day of the Crane. *Audubon,* March, pp. 46-63.

Marx, F. H. 1978. Japan's Red-Crested Cranes. *International Wildlife,* Jan., pp. 20-25.

McNulty, F. 1983. Our Far Flung Correspondence. *New Yorker,* Jan., 17, p. 88–ff.

Perrow, Charles. 1984. *Normal Accidents: Living with High Risk Technologies,* New York: Basic Books.

Ripley, S. D. 1980. View from the Castle. *Smithsonian,* Aug., p. 6.

Sauey, Ronald T. 1985, May. The Range, Status, and Winter Ecology of the Siberian Crane (*Grus leucogeranus*). Master's Thesis, Cornell University.

Schoff, Gretchen Holstein. 1991. *Reflections: The Story of Cranes,* Baraboo, WI: The International Crane Foundation.

Walkinshaw, Lawrence. 1973. *Cranes of the World,* New York: Winchester Press.

Wilder, R. 1983. Bird of Happiness. *Science Digest,* Feb., 112ff.

Witt, L. 1978. Adventure; Work of George Archibald. *People Magazine,* April 24, p. 59ff.

Zimmerman, D. K. 1981. Fragile Victory for Beauty on an Old Asian Battleground. *Smithsonian,* Oct., pp. 56–65.

# Index

artificial insemination, 26
Asian Congress, 64
Australia, 17

biological diversity, 26
breeding range, 52, 53
breeding Siberian cranes, 25

captive breeding, 16, 23
Caspian Sea, 65
China: conservation efforts in, 69, 70; Siberian cranes in, 67, 68
cold war, 28, 83, 84
conservation, reasons for, 81, 82
"Cultural Revolution," 67

"demilitarized zone," 17

education programs, 73, 78
eggs: collection of, 36, 38, 46; hatching of, 42, 44, 73; incubation of, 41, 51, 73; reintroduction after captive breeding, 23; transportation of, 31-33, 39-41, 45, 46
extinction, 13, 57, 77

genetic bank, 16
Grus leucogeranus, 12
Guinness Book of World Records, 11

Hiroshima Peace Park, 83
hunting Siberian cranes, 13, in: Afghanistan, 58-60; China, 69; India, 62; Pakistan, 60

India: conservation efforts in, 63; Keoladeo Ghana Bird Sanctuary, 18, 21, 62-65
International Crane Foundation, 22, 45, 75; captive breeding program, 17, 22, 23, 50; founding of, 15; purpose of, 15
International Crane Workshop, 63

Japan: folk traditions of, cranes in, 11, 82; Siberian cranes in, 17, 18

Korea (North and South), 17

Lake P'o-yang Hu, 69-71

migration of Siberian cranes, 57, 58, 66; distance of, 14; satellite tracking during, 66

"Operation Siberian Crane" (Operation Sterhk), 31

"Red Book," 13

Russia (Soviet Union): captive breeding program in, 50-52; financial troubles of, 81; folk tradition, cranes in, 10; Oka Nature Reserve, 50-52, 74; "Red Book," 13; United States, relations with, 16, 28, 39, 76

Siberia, 35

Siberian cranes: ancestors of, 10; breeding (see breeding Siberian cranes); call of, 9, 10, 25; dance of, 9; egg laying, 31; endangerment, causes of, 13; feeding grounds, 13; hunting of (see hunting Siberian cranes); Japanese tradition, in, 11; life span, 10, 11; migration (see, migration of Siberian cranes); nests, 12, 27; nicknames for, 12; Russian tradition, in, 10; song, 10 symbols, as, 12; wing span, 12

tundra, 12, 35, 37, 57

types of cranes: Eastern saurus crane, 17; Eurasian crane, 31; Japanese red-crowned crane, 17, 25

United States: Fish and Wildlife Service, 32; Russia, relations with, 16, 28, 39, 76

wetlands, 13, 70, 71, 77

Zhalong, 68

# About the Author

Judi Friedman is an environmental writer, educator, and activist. The author of ten books for children and numerous articles for both adults and children, she has also directed summer camps for 25 years and has presented educational programs to more than 30,000 school children. As chairperson of People's Action for Clean Energy, Ms. Friedman has worked tirelessly change to Connecticut's energy priorities.

In 1992 she received the New England Environmental Leadership award from the Lincoln Filene Center at Tufts University. Her deep concern for the environment has led her to campaign against nuclear energy and nuclear weapons. Ms. Friedman serves on the boards of Promoting Enduring Peace, the Humane Society of the United States, and EarthKind. The mother of three grown children, she lives in a wooded area of Connecticut with her beloved husband, their dog, and two horses.